FEMALE FIRSTS IN THEIR FIELDS

Air & Space

Broadcasting & Journalism

Business & Industry

Entertainment & Performing Arts

Government & Politics

Literature

Science & Medicine

Sports & Athletics

FEMALE FIRSTS IN THEIR FIELDS

SPORTS & ATHLETICS

Ann Graham Gaines

Introduction by
Roslyn Rosen

CHELSEA HOUSE PUBLISHERS
Philadelphia

Produced by P. M. Gordon Associates, Inc.
Philadelphia, Pennsylvania

Editor in Chief Stephen Reginald
Managing Editor James D. Gallagher
Production Manager Pamela Loos
Art Director Sara Davis
Director of Photography Judy L. Hasday
Senior Production Editor Lisa Chippendale
Publishing Coordinator James McAvoy

Picture research by Artemis Picture Research Group, Inc.
Cover illustration by Cliff Spohn
Cover design by Keith Trego

Frontispiece: Sheryl Swoopes

Copyright © 1999 by Chelsea House Publishers, a division of Main Line Book Co. All rights reserved. Printed and bound in the United States of America.

The Chelsea House World Wide Web site address is
http://www.chelseahouse.com

First Printing

1 3 5 7 9 8 6 4 2

Library of Congress Cataloging-in-Publication Data

Gaines, Ann Graham
　　Female firsts in their fields. Sports and athletics / Ann Graham Gaines.
　　　p. cm.
　　Includes bibliographical references and index.
　　Summary: Discusses the lives and athletic accomplishments of six women: Althea Gibson, Wilma Rudolph, Janet Guthrie, Debi Thomas, Sheryl Swoopes, and Pat Head Summitt.
　　　ISBN 0-7910-5144-7 (hardcover)
　　　1. Women athletes–United States–Biography–Juvenile literature.
　　2. Sports for women–United States–History–Juvenile literature.
　　[1. Athletes. 2. Women–Biography.] I. Title. II. Title: Sports & athletics.
　　GV697.A1G25　　1998
　　796′.082′092273–dc21
　　　　[B]　　　　　　　　　　　　　　　　　　　　　　　　98-46775
　　　　　　　　　　　　　　　　　　　　　　　　　　　　　　　CIP
　　　　　　　　　　　　　　　　　　　　　　　　　　　　　　　AC

CONTENTS

Introduction 7

CHAPTER 1
Althea Gibson 11

CHAPTER 2
Wilma Rudolph 19

CHAPTER 3
Janet Guthrie 27

CHAPTER 4
Debi Thomas 35

CHAPTER 5
Sheryl Swoopes 43

CHAPTER 6
Pat Head Summitt 53

Chronology 61

Further Reading 63

Index 64

INTRODUCTION

Roslyn Rosen

When I was a toddler, it struck me that the other people in my family's New York apartment building were different. They did not use their hands when they talked, and they did not have to watch each other speak. I had been born deaf, and I felt sorry for them because they did not know the joy of drawing pictures in the air. They could not splash ideas into the air with a jab of the finger or a wave of the hand. Not until later did I realize the downside of being deaf–I couldn't communicate directly with my grandparents and extended family members, I depended on others to make important phone calls for me, and I found life's opportunities narrower, in part because I had few deaf (let alone female) role models.

Gallaudet University in Washington, D.C., is the only college for deaf students in the world. I arrived there in September 1958. It was a haven where sign language was part of the educational process, where there were deaf professors, and where opportunities for extracurricular leadership abounded. At Gallaudet I met deaf female professionals for the first time, although there were probably not more than three or four. The president and administrators of Gallaudet were all males who could hear–typical of school administrations during those years.

In my first month at Gallaudet, I also met the man who would become my husband. My destiny was charted: major in something that I could use as a homemaker (since that would be my job), get married, have a bunch of kids, and live happily ever after. This was the expectation for women in the late 1950s and early 1960s. And I stuck to the script: I majored in art with an emphasis on education and English, got married, and had three children. My life was complete—or so I thought.

The 1960s were turbulent and thought-provoking years. The civil rights movement and the beginnings of a women's movement emphasized human rights and equality for all. I came to see how alike the issues were that faced women, people of color, and people with disabilities, in terms of human rights and respect for human differences. Multicultural studies are vital for this understanding. Changes were occurring at an accelerating rate. Those changes affected my husband and me by broadening our traditional gender roles. With my husband's support, I pursued a master's degree in education of deaf students and later a doctoral degree in education administration. From my first job as a part-time sign language teacher, I eventually joined the faculty at Gallaudet University. In 1981 I was promoted to dean of the College for Continuing Education, and in 1993, to vice president for academic affairs.

During the formative years of my career, many of my role models and mentors were deaf men who had reached positions of leadership. They hired, taught, advised, and encouraged me. There were times when I felt the effects of the "glass ceiling" (an invisible barrier that keeps women or minorities from rising any higher). Sometimes I needed to depend on my male colleagues because my access to "old boy" networks or decision makers was limited. When I became involved with the National Association of the Deaf (NAD), the world's oldest organization of deaf people, I met deaf women who became role models—Dr. Gertie Galloway was the first deaf female president of the NAD, and Marcella Meyer had founded the Greater Los Angeles Community Service of the Deaf (GLAD). In 1980 I was elected to the board of directors of the National Association of the Deaf, and in 1990, I became the second woman elected president of NAD.

When I became a dean at Gallaudet in 1981, I also became a member of the school's Council of Deans, which at the time included only two deaf deans and two female deans. I was the only deaf woman dean. The vice president was a white male, and he once commented that top administrators often build management teams in their own image. I have found that to be true. As a dean, I was the highest-ranking deaf woman at Gallaudet, and I was able to hire and help a number of young deaf female professionals within the College for Continuing Education and our regional centers around the country. In the five years that I have been vice president at Gallaudet I have added many deaf, female, and minority members to my own management team. When I was the president of NAD, I hired its first deaf female executive director, Nancy Bloch. I also encouraged two of my friends, Mabs Holcomb and Sharon Wood, to write the first deaf women history book, a source of inspiration for young deaf girls.

It is important for women who have reached the top levels of their fields to advise and help younger women to become successful. It is also important for young girls to know about the groundbreaking contributions of women who came before them. The women profiled in this series of biographies overcame many obstacles to succeed. Some had physical handicaps; others fought generations of discriminatory attitudes toward women in the workplace. The world may never provide equal opportunities for every human being, but we can all work together to improve life for the next generation.

DR. ROSLYN ROSEN is the Vice President for Academic Affairs at Gallaudet University in Washington, D.C. Dr. Rosen has served as a board member and President of the National Association of the Deaf (NAD), the oldest consumer organization in the world, and was a member of the National Captioning Institute's executive board for nine years. She is currently a board member of the World Federation of the Deaf. Dr. Rosen also wears the hats of daughter, wife, mother, and proud grandmother.

ALTHEA GIBSON

Althea Gibson was born near the small country town of Silver, South Carolina, on August 25, 1927. Her parents, Daniel and Annie Gibson, lived on a tiny five-acre farm that grew enough vegetables for the family and a little cotton. It was the time of the Great Depression, and it was hard to find a job in South Carolina. Just getting enough to eat every day was the best many people could do.

The Gibson family decided to send Althea to live in New York City with her aunt Sally, one of Annie's sisters who was doing quite well as a bootlegger in Harlem. (When the Prohibition Act of 1919 made it illegal to sell liquor, bootleggers sold smuggled or homemade liquor, often from their homes.) Aunt Sally ran her bootlegging business out of her apartment, so there were always people coming and going at all hours of the day and night.

Althea Gibson's parents also moved in with her aunt Sally, but even with so many adults around, no one had much time for Althea. She was left to find her own way on the stoops and in the streets outside of the crowded apartment house

Althea Gibson returns a serve in 1958 en route to her second straight championship at Wimbledon.

SPORTS & ATHLETICS

Remembering her own urban childhood, Gibson helps inner-city youth find their niche in athletics.

in Harlem. She grew up fast—independent, defiant, and truant. She had lost respect for her parents, and she disobeyed them often and stayed out late, sometimes overnight. She didn't like going to school—she just couldn't see any reason for it. She was often wild, playing childish pranks and committing petty thefts.

The only thing she liked more than acting out was playing games, mostly the athletic games of the street and playground. She often skipped school to play basketball or baseball in the street, right alongside the busy traffic whizzing by. She was a tough young lady on the basketball court and in the street, fighting with and sometimes beating the rough neighborhood boys her age. Her body grew lean and strong. She was lithe and quick for her 5 ft. 10 in. She weighed 140 pounds.

About one day a week in the summers, the Police Athletic League in Harlem roped off a couple of the streets in the neighborhood so kids could safely play there. Althea walked onto one such safe playground one hot afternoon in July 1941, where there was a paddleball court. Paddleball is like tennis except that a player hits the ball with a paddle instead of a racket. It's slower than tennis, but a good game for a small space. Althea played a couple of games. Her shots had the strength of a man's, and her ball sped across the court like a rocket.

Buddy Walker, an influential Harlem band leader, saw her play and was impressed. He bought her a tennis racket and gave her a chance to play in front of some wealthy black tennis fans. They were impressed with Althea's natural talent for tennis too. With their support, she began to get the best training and coaching available.

Althea Gibson was soon winning local and citywide tournaments. The trophies gave her greater self-confidence. She had found something she loved more than pranks and petty crime. Trying to be a good tennis player made her so happy with herself that she gave up being delinquent. She won the 1943 New York State Negro Girls' Singles Championship and, in 1945 and 1946, she won the National Negro Girls' Championship.

In 1949, Althea went to Florida Agricultural and Mechanical College on an athletic scholarship and played on the basketball and tennis teams. She graduated in 1953 with a bachelor of science degree.

Althea was clearly the greatest African-American tennis player in the country, but this was hardly enough for her. The feisty Althea wanted to be recognized as the best woman tennis player in the world, period. To make this happen, she would have to play in and win several of the prestigious worldwide tennis tournaments that, until that time, invited only white women to participate.

On July 1, 1950, a guest editorial by former women's tennis champion Alice Marble in the magazine *American Lawn Tennis* challenged all lovers of the game of tennis. Where was their sense of fairness? she wanted to know. She despised the efforts of the tournament committee members to keep Althea and all African-Americans from competing.

"If Althea Gibson represents a challenge to the present crop of women players," Marble wrote, "it's only fair that they should meet that challenge on the courts where tennis is played. . . . But if she is refused a chance to succeed or to fail, then there is an ineradicable mark against a game to which I have devoted most of my life, and I would be bitterly ashamed."

Her words had their desired effect. The Orange Lawn Tennis Club in South Orange, New Jersey, invited Althea to play in the 1950 Eastern Grass Court Championships. She won her first match and proved to everyone that she was more than able to compete with anyone. Later that year she reached the semifinals of the National Clay Court Championships in Chicago. In August, Lawrence Baker, the president of the U.S. Lawn Tennis Association, invited Althea to become the first African-American to play in the national championships at the West Side Tennis Club at Forest Hills, New York.

Of her historic first match at Forest Hills, Althea said, "I just wanted to get onto the court and show my talent as a tennis player. I didn't think about the racial issue or anything. I didn't think, 'Here I am the first Negro.' I was accepted as a tennis player when I walked to the court. All I thought about was how am I going to play this game and win."

Althea won her first match, 6–2, 6–2. She played her second match on the center, grandstand court against Louise Brough, the current women's Wimbledon champion and a former U.S. champion. Althea lost the first set, 6–1, but regained her composure and won the second set, 6–3, with her strong serve and fine basic tennis skills. The two women had begun the third and deciding set of the match when lightning flashed, signaling the coming of a summer thunderstorm. Althea fell behind, 3–0, but surged back to tie the match, then forged ahead at 7–6.

The lightning and thunder grew closer. Althea needed to win only one more game to make tennis history. The storm hit Forest Hills. Players, officials, and fans all ran for cover. The match was postponed. At that moment, a lightning bolt struck the top of the stadium and knocked a stone eagle decoration to the ground. Nature itself seemed to be doing its part to change the game of tennis. Whether Althea Gibson won or not, the strength of her play ensured that competitive tennis from that moment on would embrace all races.

The match continued the next day, but the spell was broken. Althea remembered, "There is no doubt in my mind, or in anybody else's that the delay was the worst thing that could have happened to me. It gave me a whole evening—and the next morning, too, for that matter—to think about the match. By the time I got through reading the morning newspapers I was a nervous wreck."

The match was over in 11 minutes. Louise Brough won the decisive game and tied the match at 7–7, then won the next two games for the match. Still, Althea had changed tennis. The year after that loss, 1951, Althea was the first African-American invited to play at Wimbledon, the English national tennis championship. She reached the quarterfinals before she was defeated. She lost in the finals of the U.S. Indoor Championship to Nancy Chaffee. In 1953 she lost to Maureen Connolly at Forest Hills, and in 1954, she was defeated by Helen Perez. Despite these losses, Althea continued to play well. She was rated seventh among women in the United States in 1953, 13th in 1954, and eighth in 1955, but she was not winning the big tournaments, and she began to think of retirement.

In the fall of 1955, Althea was named as one of four "goodwill ambassadors of tennis" and sent on

To go with her 1957 Wimbledon trophy, Gibson receives a congratulatory kiss from her defeated opponent, Darlene Hard.

After her historic triumph at Wimbledon, Gibson is honored with a ticker-tape parade in New York in July 1957. Riding with her is Manhattan borough president Hulan Jack.

a tour of Asia. This tour was exactly what Althea needed to learn how to win the big ones. She won both the Indian National and Asiatic Women's Singles championships. In 1956, she helped win the French indoor doubles in February, continued with seven tournament wins in France, Monte Carlo, and Italy in the next several months, and won the French National Women's Championship in May. She then won several tournaments in England. When she was eliminated by Shirley Fry, the number one seed (top woman player) at Wimbledon in July, it was the first tournament in 15 tries that she did not win.

The next year, 1957, was the best year in Althea's tennis life. She was rated the favorite to win Wimbledon. She defeated Darlene Hard in the finals, 6–3, 6–2, playing in 100-degree afternoon heat. "At last, at last," was all Althea could say as the match ended. She received a silver tray from the queen of England as her prize. She was the first black athlete, man or woman, to win Wimbledon.

When Althea returned to the United States, she was given a ticker-tape parade down the streets of New York. Two months later, she won the U.S. Open at Forest Hills. She repeated as champion of both Wimbledon and Forest Hills in 1958. Althea had achieved her goals. She was clearly the best in the world. And because of her, it was a bigger tennis world, too.

Althea gave up tennis in 1958 and later became a leader on the women's professional golf tour for a short while. She married for a brief time, but the marriage ended in divorce. She suffered several strokes and illnesses that have kept her from recent public appearances. She lives today in East Orange, New Jersey, surrounded by her trophies and her memories.

WILMA RUDOLPH

Wilma Rudolph was in a hurry since before she was born. She arrived two months ahead of schedule and weighed only four-and-a-half pounds when she was born on June 23, 1940, in a small country town, St. Bethlehem, Tennessee. When Wilma was still an infant, her parents, Ed and Blanche Rudolph, moved with her to Clarksville, Tennessee. Ed worked as a porter, and Blanche worked as a cleaning lady for several families in the town.

Wilma seemed to catch every childhood disease in existence. She had two serious illnesses when she was about four—double pneumonia and scarlet fever. Just as she was recovering, her left leg became stiff. The ankle locked with the foot turned inward. It was polio, the doctors said. A viral disease that affected many children in the 1940s, polio came in a wave, usually during the summer, passed through a town, city, or state and moved on. Not every year, but three or four times in the decade of the 1940s, polio passed through the United States. By 1955, polio had killed or crippled over 357,000 people in the United States, mostly children.

A sickly child, Wilma Rudolph conquered polio and other serious diseases to become a track champion.

SPORTS & ATHLETICS

In overcoming the many obstacles she faced, Rudolph received a great deal of support from her family. Here she is greeted after her Olympic triumphs by her mother, Blanche (left); her father, Ed; and her younger sister Charlene (right).

Polio produced a very high fever, as the body fought the rapidly multiplying virus. The body usually won, but the high fever often destroyed the nerve connections between the muscles of the body. These muscles could not then receive the brain's instructions to move. They remained stiff and paralyzed.

The only treatment seemed to be regular exercise of the muscles in the paralyzed parts of the body. Massage and exercise could bring paralyzed muscles back to useful life. But it took many months, often years. And it took people willing to do the massage and exercise for the polio victim. Often these exercises were conducted underwater, because the water supports the muscles and makes them easier to move. Very slowly, day by day, the repeated exercising of the muscles could show the body how to rebuild the damaged nerve connections.

Luckily for Wilma, there was a lot of love among the 22 children in the Rudolph household. There was always someone around the house who could massage her leg—and at the same time fill her in on the latest neighborhood gossip.

The nearest place for water exercises was a hospital in Nashville, 45 miles away. At great sacrifice—for the family never had any extra money—Wilma and her mom would take the bus to Nashville every week for these special exercises. Every day after cleaning houses, Wilma's mom would sit and gently massage Wilma's stiff leg and they would talk about life, or the weather, or supper. Wilma was a naturally happy girl, and polio did not change her positive outlook.

Until she was eight years old, Wilma could not go to school because she could not walk. Slowly, the massage and weekly therapy at the hospital began to show results. Wilma was fitted with a steel brace for her left leg, with a special shoe for her twisted foot. With the aid of this brace Wilma began to take a few steps. It was a wonderful time for her—with the new brace she could go to school!

She enrolled at Cobb Elementary School. She didn't mind too much that kids at school made fun of her, or that she couldn't take part in the fun at recess. All of that would come with hard work, and Wilma was ready for hard work. She wanted to run and play like the rest of the kids.

Some of her brothers put a basketball hoop up in the yard and Wilma began to practice. She grew to love the game. Her body grew stronger every day as she practiced repeatedly. By the time she was 11 years old, Wilma knew that she could walk without her brace.

One Sunday morning, Wilma waited outside church while everyone else went in for the service. She unbuckled the heavy brace and left it at the steps to the church door. Slowly, one tiny step at a time, Wilma walked down the aisle and proudly took her place with the rest of her family in one of the front pews. The songs of praise raised for the wonders of God were especially sweet and loud that morning. Soon Wilma and her mom mailed the brace back to the hospital for someone else to use—Wilma no longer needed it.

At 13, Wilma wanted to play basketball on the team at Burt High School in Clarksville. The Burt basketball coach, Clinton Gray, said no. He thought she was too sickly, too fragile—she might be hurt. He badly wanted Wilma's older sister to play for the team, however. Wilma's dad, Ed Rudolph, decided that the coach would have to accept both girls for the team or neither would play. The coach finally agreed to let Wilma play.

Wilma became a star for Burt. She scored 803 points in 25 games her sophomore year. Coach Gray nicknamed her "Skeeter," because she was always buzzing around the basketball court like a mosquito. Wilma became an all-state basketball player when she was 15 years old. But as good as she was at basketball, she was even better at track. In her three final years of high school, Wilma never lost a race in competition. This girl who could not walk six years earlier ran like a deer.

Ed Temple, the women's track coach at Tennessee State A & I University, thought that Wilma could become a great international track star. He offered her a full, four-year scholarship to study and run track at the university when she graduated from high school in 1957. She would be the first member of her family to attend college.

While Wilma was still in high school, she and Coach Temple decided that she was already good enough to run in the 1956 Olympic Games, which were being held in Melbourne, Australia. So she went to Seattle, Washington, to try out for the U.S. track team. She tied for first place in her qualifying race, the 200-meter dash. She had made the team.

The entire U.S. Olympic team traveled around the world to Melbourne to compete with all of the other nations of the world. Wilma did not get a medal in the 200-meter dash; she finished third in the semifinal race. But she also ran on the women's 400-meter relay team, which finished third. Wilma came home to Clarksville with an Olympic bronze medal—she was just 16 years old.

That fall, Wilma began to study elementary education at Tennessee State A & I University.

Wilma was sick throughout the 1958 track season and did not run at all. The next year, at a dual meet between the United States and Russia, Wilma pulled a muscle in her left thigh and could not compete. The next year, 1960, was another Olympic year. Wilma knew in her heart that she could win a gold medal this time. Unfortunately, she had to have her tonsils removed and took a long time recovering from the operation.

But when August and the Olympics arrived, she was ready. A reporter for *Time* magazine described how she looked during her races. "Running for gold medal glory, Miss Rudolph regularly got away to good starts with her arms pumping in classic style, then smoothly shifted gears to a flowing stride that made the rest of the pack seem to be churning on a treadmill."

Three times that summer in Rome, Italy, Wilma ran for gold. She won the 100-meter dash by more than three yards for an unofficial world record of 11.0 seconds. In the 200-meter dash, Wilma set an Olympic record, 23.2 seconds, in her first qualifying race. She already had the world record time of 22.9 seconds in the event. She went on to win the gold medal against strong competition.

She won her third gold medal by running the

Rudolph shows her "flowing stride" during training for the 1960 Olympics.

SPORTS & ATHLETICS

Rudolph waves to the crowd after receiving her Olympic gold medal for the 200-meter event. Sharing the podium are Jutta Heine of Germany (right), who took the silver medal, and bronze medalist Dorothy Hyman of Great Britain.

anchor leg (the last leg) of the 400-meter women's relay. The team, composed of her teammates from Tennessee State University, ran in a world record time of 44.4 seconds. Wilma became the first woman to win three medals in track at a single Olympic Games.

She was a heroine. Thousands of fans mobbed her as she continued to compete in track meets in Europe after the Olympics. In Berlin, Germany, the pressing crowds stole the shoes off her feet. When she returned to Clarksville, a parade, a carnival, and a dinner were held in her honor. In 1961, she was voted the female athlete of the year in the United States and won the James E. Sullivan Memorial trophy as the country's best amateur athlete.

While she enjoyed the success, she found that fame had its negative side. "[Some of my friends] bend over backwards to please me. But that's not the same as being friends and it's certainly not the way I want it."

Wilma retired from amateur athletics in 1963. She received a bachelor of arts degree in elementary education and married Robert Eldridge, her college sweetheart, and they had a family. She became a second-grade teacher and a high school track coach in Clarksville, at the same schools she had attended as a child. In 1977, she published her life story, *Wilma,* and it was made into a television movie.

Wilma Rudolph died on November 24, 1994, in Nashville, Tennessee, from brain cancer. She has been elected a member of the U.S. Olympic Hall of Fame and the U.S. Track and Field Hall of Fame.

JANET GUTHRIE

Almost from the time she could walk, Janet Guthrie was a smart girl who enjoyed a challenge. Her father, William Lain Guthrie, said that "when she was about three, I once told her, 'If you hurt yourself doing what I'm telling you not to do, I'll give you a spanking anyway.' She looked up and said, 'Doesn't sound right to me.'"

Her dad was an airplane pilot, and Janet's earliest goal was to fly an airplane just like he did. Later she nearly became an astronaut. Fast machines must have been in her blood. In 1977, when she was 39, Janet Guthrie became the first woman to drive in the Indianapolis 500.

Born on March 7, 1938, in Iowa City, Iowa, she was the oldest of five kids. Her dad operated a small airport on the edge of town. When he later took a job as a pilot for Eastern Airlines, he moved the family to Miami, Florida, which is where Janet grew up.

Janet says that she always enjoyed challenges. Learning to fly a plane takes a long time—she had to get familiar with many different controls and gauges and do a lot of studying

Janet Guthrie acknowledges cheers after finishing in the top 10 in the 1978 Indianapolis 500.

in physics, math, and geography, to understand and use them all. She took lessons with an instructor pilot, who would handle the take-off and then give the controls of the plane to Janet, so that she could practice and develop a feel for flying. The instructor would again take over to bring the plane in for a landing. Janet actually flew an airplane for the first time—with the instructor beside her—when she was 13 years old.

Her first "solo" flight, when she took off, flew, and landed the plane entirely by herself, came when she was 16. At 16 she also trained to jump from an airplane and made her first parachute jump. The following year she had her commercial pilot's license. By the time she was 21, she had piloted an airplane in flight for more than 400 hours. She had experience flying more than 20 different kinds of airplane. At this point she decided she wanted to become the first woman astronaut.

Janet attended the University of Michigan beginning in 1957, the same year that the Russians launched Sputnik, the first satellite. She graduated with a bachelor of science degree in physics in 1960. (She called learning physics an exciting adventure too.) She got a job with the Republic Aviation Corporation in Farmingdale, Long Island, New York, as an aerospace research and development engineer.

Janet felt confident that she could become one of the first female astronauts because she was already both a pilot and an engineer, skills an astronaut needed. She was one of four women accepted for the first scientist-astronaut program of NASA, but later she was eliminated from the program because she did not have her doctorate degree in science.

This was a disappointment, but Janet had several other challenges in her life, so she didn't spend long moping. One of her favorite hobbies was her sports

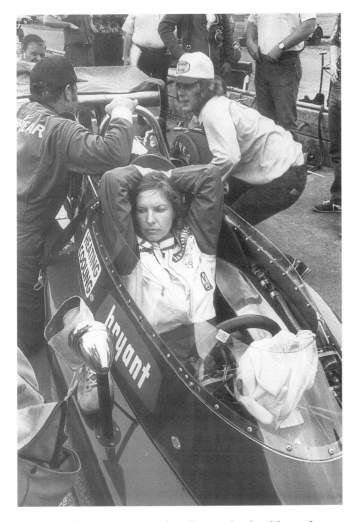

Resented by some for entering a male-dominated sport, Guthrie has a lot to ponder as she awaits the beginning of a race in the 1970s.

car. Her first year out of college, she had bought an old, classy Jaguar XK 120 on her $125.00 a month salary. Long Island, where Janet was living, is a popular center for the gymkhana, an automobile competition that calls for nimble handling rather than brute speed. Janet soon fell in love with weaving the old Jaguar around obstacles and pylons in many local weekend events.

And she was good at it. After she won the 1962 Women's Gymkhana Championship of Long Island,

SPORTS & ATHLETICS

Guthrie rises from the driver's seat in 1977 after becoming the first woman ever to qualify for the Indianapolis 500.

she attended a sports car driving school at Limerock, Connecticut. Gordon McKenzie, a veteran driver at Limerock, thought she was a natural. He was impressed by her combination of daring and care, as well as by her cool mechanical skills under pressure. He asked her if she had ever thought of driving as a professional.

Janet jumped at the chance. She traded in her old Jaguar XK 120 for a racing version, the Jaguar XK 140, and over the next couple of months rebuilt the engine and learned how to set up the steering and suspension for different kinds of racing. Like everything she found challenging, racing called for using the mind and the body, the whole person. She later said of her love for auto racing, "I know of no other activity that calls upon you to extend yourself 100 percent on all levels—physical, emotional, intellectual, spiritual."

When she attended a Sports Car Club of America driving school for racers in 1963, there were no women in professional auto racing. That year she drove in 13 races, including one at the famous Watkins Glen racing course in New York. In 1964, she finished second in her class and fifth overall in the six-hour road race at Watkins Glen. From 1966 through 1971, she was sponsored by the Ring-Free Oil Company; she placed in the top three at such prestigious races as Daytona, Sebring, and Watkins Glen.

So far Janet had raced only in sports car races, under the sponsorship of the Sports Car Club of America. Now she wanted to compete with the male racers who drove the fastest, most powerful racing machines in the world on such oval, high-speed tracks as Indianapolis and Trenton, under the sponsorship of the U.S. Auto Club (USAC). The famous Indianapolis 500 race each Memorial Day is a USAC event.

Guthrie joins other women's sports figures in 1982 to celebrate the 10th anniversary of Title IX, the law prohibiting sex discrimination in federally supported educational institutions.

One person who believed in her was Rolla Vollstedt, an Indianapolis race car team owner from Oregon. He telephoned Janet: Would she like to drive one of two cars he was preparing for the Indianapolis 500 race for 1976? She began to train. At secret tests on an oval course near Los Angeles, California, in February 1976, Janet averaged 172.58 mph and had a top lap speed of 196 mph. These were fast, competitive times. She was ready to race with the big boys.

Although Janet did not get to race at Indianapolis that year, she did race Memorial Day weekend at the Charlotte World 600-mile stock car race—the first woman to race in an event sponsored by the National Association for Stock Car Racing,

NASCAR. In NASCAR races, drivers use highly modified American passenger cars, like Fords and Pontiacs, to race oval tracks like Indy. Janet ran well and finished 15th. She ran in five other NASCAR events in 1976, finished 15th twice, and earned $8,179.

The rest of the 1976 season Janet raced at Indy-like races in New Jersey, New York, and Michigan. She drove well in all of them, but her car broke down each time, twice with gear-box failures and once with a flat tire. There were no breakthrough wins. She didn't even complete a race—but she and her crew gained valuable experience.

In 1976, at the race in Trenton, New Jersey, some people in the crowd shouted, "Go back to the kitchen!" when they saw Janet on the track. Until a 1972 court decision forbade it, women had been excluded from all Indianapolis-style racing. There were no women drivers, mechanics, pit crews, timers, owners, or reporters—there were no women in USAC racing at all.

On May 7, 1977, Janet became the first woman to race at the Indianapolis racetrack. She did it in real style, setting a record of 191 mph in her first qualifying run. On May 10, during a practice lap, she crashed into the wall of the course at over 180 mph. Fortunately, she was not hurt. The car was damaged only slightly and was repaired in time for the race. Janet raced well early in the race, but she completed only 27 laps before the car again broke down with gear-box problems.

Back at Indianapolis again in 1978, she qualified in Number 27, a faster version of the Rolla Vollstedt car that she had driven the year before. This time Janet had the 15th fastest time in qualifying, so she started in 15th place for the race. She drove well the entire race and finished ninth—the first woman to race at Indianapolis and the first woman to finish the race. Her ninth-place finish is still the highest place ever achieved by a woman in the race—just another exciting challenge answered by Janet Guthrie.

Guthrie has since retired from professional racing, but she remains active with passions for ballet, classical music, cooking, and picnicking on Long Island. In 1998, she was voted into the International Motor Sports Hall of Fame.

DEBI THOMAS

Before she was even old enough to go to school, Debi Thomas had two ambitions: she wanted to be a doctor, and she wanted to win an Olympic medal as an ice skater. Don't ever let anyone tell you dreams—even big dreams—can't come true. Today Debi is on her way to becoming an orthopedic surgeon, and in 1988 she became the first African-American to win an Olympic medal in ice skating.

Debi Thomas was born on March 25, 1967, in Poughkeepsie, New York. She grew up in San Jose, California. As a child, she said, "I used to make my mom buy me a doctor's kit; I didn't want the nurse's kit." When she was four years old, her mother took her to see an ice-skating show starring Mr. Frick, the "King of Trick Skating." Debi fell in love with Mr. Frick's fancy turns and jumps on the ice and begged her mom for skates. She had her first ice-skating lesson when she was five and immediately decided she wanted to skate in the Olympics and win a medal.

Becoming a good enough athlete to compete in the Olympics takes years of hard work. Not just Debi, but her whole family, had to make the commitment. Her mom, Jan-

Debi Thomas skates her short program at the 1988 Olympics.

ice, was a computer programmer and divorced from Debi's dad. Debi's lessons and equipment cost a lot. Her father and grandparents chipped in, but Debi remembers wearing tight-fitting secondhand skates and costumes that were sewn at home. Her mother drove 3,000 miles a month taking Debi to and from lessons. It was a struggle.

When she was 10 years old, Debi began to take lessons from Alex McGowan, a professional skating coach who was impressed by her hard work and the way she demanded excellence of herself. Debi had the desire and the patience to learn the basic moves of skating, which are so important when judges score a skater's performance. She learned to smoothly and gracefully switch from skating forward to skating backward. She learned to turn on one skate so that she left a perfect circle in the ice as she moved. And she learned the jumps—the spectacular part of skating. She was a strong girl, and she could perform triple jumps—making three complete revolutions in the air, then landing on the ice as lightly as a feather.

From the start of her training Debi performed well at local competitions. When she was only 12, she won a silver medal in the U.S. junior Nationals.

With more training and practice, Debi thought she would be able to win the junior Worlds competition scheduled for the next year. To give her more time to skate, she and her mom decided that Debi could skate full-time and do the schoolwork for the eighth grade at home. That turned out to be a bad idea. Debi finished fourth in the regional skating tournament—she didn't even qualify for the national competition.

From then on, Debi concentrated equally on her skating and her education. She continued to get better at skating, and she did so well in high school that she was admitted to three of the country's top colleges: Stanford, Harvard, and Princeton. She chose nearby Stanford University in California, where she studied science to prepare for medical school after college graduation.

Even though combining school and skating was hard, Debi thought that concentrating on skating alone didn't always work. "A lot of people think it'll be too difficult to train and go to school full time," she said, "but I think it'll help me from frying my brain. You have to be dedicated to be a skater, but you can really wreck yourself by thinking 'skating, skating, skating.' I know too many skaters who don't get the gold medals or the big skating contracts and their lives are over. I want to leave this sport willingly."

But her first year at Stanford University proved too stressful. She had no time for fun or friends. She gained 15 pounds, became depressed, and tore up her application for the National Championships that were to be held in Uniondale, New York, that year. After a short vacation with lots of rest, she decided to compete in the Nationals after all, even though the event was only five weeks later. She sent off her application and devoted herself to training.

In February 1986, Debi won the National Championship, defeating Tiffany Chin. She completed five

As a youngster Debi always demanded excellence of herself, both in her skating and in her schoolwork.

triple jumps in a wonderful performance. She described her thoughts as she went out on the ice and skated her way to the championship: "I told myself, 'All your friends are watching, and if you don't skate well, they're not going to know what to say except that your dress looked nice.'

"The announcer called my name, and I heard a roar. It was just exhilarating, and I thought, 'I'll take the jumps one at a time.' I landed my first triple, then the second, the one I'd messed up in practice. My fourth is a hard one for me, and my coach had wanted me to take it out, but I said no. I came down, and when I found I was still standing, well, my mouth dropped open. I thought, 'Where did that come from?' I was having a ball."

In Switzerland in March 1986, the next month, Debi became the first African-American woman to win the World Championships. She defeated Katarina Witt of Germany, who had held the title since 1984. In the audience that night was Mr. Frick, the skater who had inspired Debi when she was a little girl. At the medal ceremony after the competition, Mr. Frick presented Debi with a special bouquet of flowers.

In the national competition the next year, 1987, Debi pulled muscles in both of her legs and lost her national title, but she turned her attention to the Olympics, scheduled for Calgary, Canada, in 1988. Debi knew that a winning performance in the Olympics would require even more training, so she dropped out of college to skate.

She was already one of the most athletic skaters in the world—five successful triple jumps in one routine proved that. What needed work was the artistic side of her skating. She went to work with Mikhail Baryshnikov, the famous Russian ballet dancer. He helped her to hold her hands and body

A natural athlete, Thomas worked hard to add grace and beauty to her skating.

in graceful positions, and to move her body in time with the changes in the music. Debi's routine became more and more like a ballet dance on ice—beautiful turns and twirls along with her spectacular jumps. Debi felt that she was ready.

Everyone knew that the real competition for the 1988 Olympic gold medal in skating was between Debi and Katarina Witt. At Calgary, they both skated well—in fact, they had both chosen the same music for their routines. On Debi's first triple jump, she made a tiny mistake: She landed on both feet, instead of just on one. Her error distracted her attention, and she skated well but not her best.

SPORTS & ATHLETICS

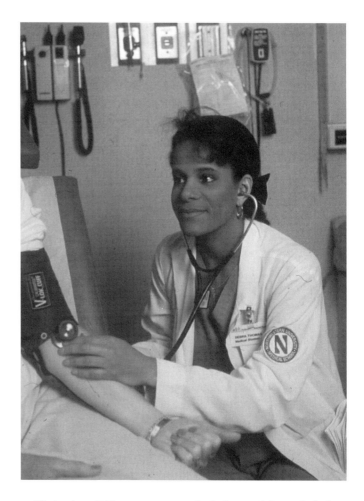

Pursuing her second great goal, Thomas attended medical school and became a physician.

Katarina Witt was awarded the gold medal, but Debi won the bronze, and became the first African-American to win an Olympic medal in ice skating.

The next month, Debi competed in the World Championships and again finished with the bronze medal.

She married Brian Vanden Hogen, a student at the University of Colorado whom she met while training for the Olympics. The marriage lasted only three years. She graduated from Stanford University in 1991. For the next four years, Debi toured with the professional ice-skating company Stars on Ice.

But she could not ignore the other great goal of her life, a career in medicine. She decided to retire from skating and concentrate on becoming a doctor. The next semester Debi began her medical studies at Northwestern University Medical School near Chicago, Illinois. She married Chris Bequette, a lawyer, and graduated from medical school in June 1997. The next month she gave birth to a son, Luc. As a resident in a hospital, Debi is now in another phase of her medical training. She's well on her way to being the orthopedic surgeon she has dreamed about becoming for so many years.

But Debi Thomas has never been satisfied with having just one goal in her life. Today she's looking ahead to another great challenge. "There's this little voice in my head," she says, "and it keeps saying, 'Apply to the astronaut program when you finish your residency.'"

Tenley Albright, a Boston surgeon who was a women's ice-skating champion in the 1950s, says Debi's life is a good one for anyone to model their own life after. "What Debi has done is encourage kids to get into a sport they love and show that they can have a career or other interests as well. It's a wonderful message. I call her balanced both on the ice and in life."

SHERYL SWOOPES

In June 1995, Women's National Basketball Association star Sheryl Swoopes signed a multimillion-dollar contract with Nike to endorse a new line of shoes, the Air Swoopes. In 1997, two months after she gave birth to a son, Jordan, she was scoring more than 20 points a game for the Houston Comets, who won the WNBA league championship on August 30. She was 24 years old.

Born on March 25, 1971, in Brownfield, Texas, a small town on the flat prairie lands of the Texas Panhandle, Sheryl was the only daughter in a close-knit family with three brothers and her mom, Louise. Louise Swoopes worked three jobs to support the family, and there wasn't a lot of money for babysitters or extra toys. The kids learned to watch out for each other and to entertain themselves.

James and Earl, Sheryl's two older brothers, put up a bike wheel rim in the backyard to serve as a hoop, and the kids played a lot of one-on-one basketball with each other. Sheryl quickly learned to use her strength and quickness when it was her turn. Her brothers treated her just like one of the

Sheryl Swoopes wins fans not just with her scoring, but also with her presence on and off the court.

boys, and they were happy to take advantage of any mistakes she made from being too timid.

Later, Sheryl gave credit to these neighborhood games with the boys for making her a superior ball handler. "It helps to play with the guys; they're so much more physical than girls are. Once you go out and you play with guys, and you get in a situation with girls, you think, 'Well, if I scored on that guy, I know I can score on her.'"

At Brownfield High School, Sheryl sparked the women's basketball team to three Texas State High School Championships with her aggressive, confident play. In 1989, her senior year, she averaged 26 points, 5 assists, and 14 rebounds a game. She was named a high school All-American and the Texas Girls High School Basketball Player of the Year. She got a scholarship to play for the University of Texas at Austin, but she was there only three days; she was too homesick to stay. She returned to the Lubbock area near her home and enrolled in a junior college, South Plains College at Levelland.

Her freshman year at South Plains, she led the basketball team to a 29-win season. She was named to the junior college All-American team. The next year, Sheryl was named Most Valuable Player of the conference championship finals. She set 28 records at South Plains, including an incredible 139 steals in her sophomore year.

When she graduated from junior college, Sheryl enrolled at Texas Tech University in Lubbock. Her basketball coach there, Marsha Sharp, said the Texas Tech team could compete on a national scale because of Sheryl. "She'll be a legend in women's basketball, but not just because of her play. She has the charisma that the crowd loves."

In the two years Sheryl played for the Lady Red Raiders at Texas Tech, the team compiled a 58–8

Swoopes prepares to score two of her 31 points in the 1993 NCAA semifinal game. The next day she poured in 47 to lead Texas Tech to the national championship.

record. Her first year, 1992, she led the conference in steals (110) and ranked second in free-throw percentage (.808), third in assists (152), fourth in rebound average (8.9), and fifth in blocked shots (32). Her senior year, 1993, was even more dramatic. She won the conference's Most Valuable Player Award as she led the Lady Red Raiders to a second Southwest Conference championship.

On April 4, 1993, in the final game of the Women's National Basketball Championship, televised across the United States, Sheryl scored 47 points for Texas Tech in their close win over Ohio State University, 84–82. Sheryl's mom, Louise, and two of her brothers had driven the family car 19 hours from Brownfield, Texas, to Atlanta, Georgia, to sit in the stands and see Sheryl's championship performance.

SPORTS & ATHLETICS

Swoopes (right) hugs teammate Ruthie Bolton, crying for joy, as the U.S. team wins the Olympic gold medal in 1996.

The head coach of the Ohio State team talked later about Sheryl's play. "You don't appreciate Sheryl Swoopes until you have to stop her. We had made some plans to contain her. We wanted to rotate people on her, which we did. We wanted her to work hard for her shots and not just get lay-ups. We also tried trapping her when she had the ball. But she answered everything we tried."

Sheryl set 10 records in that final championship series, including most points in a game (47) and highest scoring average (35.4 points).

For years, many men who play college basketball have gone on to professional basketball careers with teams in the National Basketball Association, playing alongside NBA stars like Julius Irving, Magic Johnson, and Michael Jordan. But until 1997, no league for professional women's basketball had succeeded in the United States. By the 1990s, however, the exciting new style of women's play was drawing large crowds and enthusiastic television audiences. Sheryl's exposure on national television and her ready smile and commanding presence on the court had made her popular with thousands of young girls around the country who played her aggressive, fun style of basketball.

In June 1995, Sheryl signed an endorsement contract with the Kellogg cereal company and later in the year signed a lucrative contract with the Nike shoe company to endorse a new line, the Air Swoopes. Ten years earlier Michael Jordan had signed a similar deal to introduce Nike's popular Air Jordans.

On June 17, 1995, Sheryl married Eric Jackson, her high school sweetheart.

On August 4, 1996, Sheryl was one of the 11-member U.S. women's basketball team that defeated the women's team from Brazil, 111–87, and won the gold medal in the Centennial Olympics in Atlanta. Almost everyone on that talented team went on to star in the newly forming pro league, the WNBA. The people organizing the WNBA knew that they needed to establish a working league of teams, competing with each other on a high professional level of play, and a couple of real star personalities to attract fan support. On October 23, 1996, the first players of the new women's league, Rebecca Lobo and Sheryl Swoopes, two of the biggest of the Olympic stars, were signed to play in the new WNBA. They were soon followed by Olympic teammate Lisa Leslie.

SPORTS & ATHLETICS

Swoopes shows her poise on the Late Show with David Letterman *in 1996.*

The next week the new league announced the eight cities that were to host the first teams in the league: Charlotte, North Carolina; Cleveland, Ohio; Houston, Texas; Los Angeles, California; New York City; Phoenix, Arizona; Sacramento, California; and Salt Lake City, Utah. On February 27, 1997, the WNBA held its elite draft for 16 signed veteran players. Sheryl was chosen by the Houston Comets. On April 28, 1997, the WNBA held its draft for college players and unsigned veterans.

On June 21, 1997, the inaugural WNBA season began.

Eric and Sheryl were determined from the start

Mom can do it: Swoopes returns to practice with the WNBA Comets a month after the birth of her son Jordan in 1997.

of their marriage to stay together as a family unit, even if they could not live a traditional family life. Sheryl had to be away, often for weeks at a time, on a grueling basketball schedule that took her around the country, and sometimes around the world. So she and Eric decided to take their family on the road too. They began to travel together, Eric as her weight trainer, bodyguard, and part-time coach.

On June 25, 1997, four days after the season opened, they became a traveling family of three. Sheryl Swoopes gave birth to a healthy 7-pound, 9-ounce son, Jordan (of course, named after Michael Jordan). The day after he was born, Sheryl asked her doctors if it was all right to return to training. Six weeks later, she played five minutes for the Houston Comets that she said "felt more like 15 or 20." But she was in better shape than she'd expected, she said. "I'm amazed at myself. I'm not as far away from where I want to be as I thought."

Today Sheryl and Eric welcome help from the rest of the family. Louise attends as many games as she can and helps watch Jordan until halftime, when Sheryl breast-feeds him in a private room near the team locker room.

Once she began to get some playing time, Sheryl quickly regained her wind and timing. By August, as the race for the title intensified, Sheryl was contributing more than 20 points a game. On August 30, 1997, Sheryl's team, the Houston Comets, won the league championship. Their smothering defense beat the New York Liberty by a score of 65–51.

The season was a popular success with the crowds, and the second year the WNBA added two new teams—in Washington, D.C., and Detroit, Michigan. Seven women in the league besides Sheryl have children. Her teammate on the Houston Comets, Yolanda Moore, is the mother of two.

Sheryl wrote a popular children's book, *Bounce Back*, with Greg Brown, in which she used stories from her own life to convince young readers to stick to their goals. She also put out a videotape, "Swoopes on Hoops," that tells young viewers why she constantly strives to better herself as both a basketball player and a person.

Today Sheryl Swoopes has her multimillion-dollar contract for Air Swoopes and has appeared in Nike's television commercials for the sneakers. One of the best paid and most talented of the new superstars in women's professional sports, Sheryl Swoopes is also an exceptional example of a modern working mother.

PAT HEAD SUMMITT

Pat Summitt, who coaches the Lady Vols at the University of Tennessee, is one of the best basketball coaches ever—man or woman. She didn't get there by luck or accident. She has been strong and determined all of her life—determined to succeed at everything, stubborn enough to overcome all of the obstacles that life has put in her path. She never missed a day of school from the first through the eighth grades. She overcame a badly torn knee ligament to bring home a silver Olympic medal. Today she trails only John Wooden of UCLA for the most national basketball championships (6), and she trails only Jody Conradt of the University of Texas for the most wins in an entire career.

Patricia Sue Head was the fourth child and first daughter of Richard and Hazel Head. Her family called her "Trish." Linda, the fifth child, was born when Trish was seven. Trish and her brothers, Tommy, Kenneth, and Charles, helped their parents on the family dairy and tobacco farm near Clarksville, Tennessee. Richard Head not only worked the family farm but ran a grocery store six miles away, built houses, and

Coach Pat Summitt gets the spoils of victory—the net—after her Tennessee team wins the 1989 national championship.

served as the county water commissioner and on the county court. Hazel mowed the lawn when she had time free from the other duties of a farm mother. When someone at the church died, Hazel was the first to show up with a couple of cooked meals to help out.

Trish learned early the value of hard work. Everyone had their chores to do every day on the farm, and when they finished those, they helped with the big jobs that required everyone to pitch in. By the time she was 10 or 11, Trish was driving a tractor to rake and bale the hay crop and plow the field. She set and harvested tobacco plants with the rest of the family, and she raised calves as a part of the local 4-H program at school.

Of course, there was school. Richard Head did not believe in missing school. And there was church. Every Sunday when the doors opened at Mount Carmel United Methodist Church near Ashland City, the Head family was waiting.

There were no other children to play with, because the neighbors lived too far away for daily visits. To give his children some fun on the farm, Richard Head put up a basket and some lights on one wall of the 100-foot-long hayloft in the barn so that they could play basketball. For years, the four older Head kids played two-on-two basketball in the hayloft. Trish and her oldest brother, Tommy, would play against Kenneth and Charles. It was an even match, according to Charles. "I reckon she was just one of the boys. In that hayloft, she was right in the middle of us. That's what made her tough."

Trish played basketball well, but the high school in Clarksville did not have a girls' team. So Richard Head moved the family into an old house near the family grocery store in nearby Henrietta, just over the line in Cheatham County. That way, Trish could attend high school in Ashland City, which did have a girls' basketball team.

The Heads did not allow Trish to date until she was 16, and she did not go out for pizza until she was a senior in high school. Trish has said that she and her brothers and sisters were too afraid to rebel against their parents. "Rebel? Are you kidding? A lot of discipline came as a result of fear. We had to get our own switch out of the yard. And if you got a little one, Mama would get her own. I hated that."

On her 16th birthday, she was supposed to go with some friends to a local country club for a party, but it started to rain and there was still a lot of hay left in the field that would be ruined if it got wet. Richard Head would not let Trish go to her birthday party until all of the hay was in the barn. "I think I wound up getting in trouble with my dad that day. I was so mad I wasn't paying attention. I think I got a switch that day, and it wasn't birthday licks."

After high school, Trish went to college at the University of Tennessee at Martin, where the officials called her "Pat." She was just shy enough not to correct them. (Her family still calls her "Trish.") She became a star basketball player on the college's team. In 1974, her senior year in college, she tore the anterior cruciate ligament in her left knee. It couldn't have happened at a worse time. Women's basketball was scheduled to become an Olympic event at the Montreal Olympics in 1976, and Pat wanted passionately to be a part of that team.

The orthopedic surgeon who examined the knee told her to forget about the Olympics; she could never recover in time to play. Fix the knee, Richard Head told the surgeon, and she'll play. Richard Head did not believe much in physical limitations either.

SPORTS & ATHLETICS

Olympic glory: members of the U.S. women's Olympic team carry Coach Summitt off the court after winning the gold medal in 1984. Summitt had played on the silver-medal squad in 1976.

In 1975, Pat entered graduate school at the university, studying for a master's degree. She also taught four freshman courses in physical education and took a job as the assistant coach of the women's basketball team. To rehabilitate her knee after the operation, she was supposed to lose 15 pounds and work out twice a day. She began her day with a three-mile run at 6 A.M., followed by weight training, teaching physical education classes, taking her own graduate classes in sports administration, coaching the basketball team, then returning to the gym for two hours of her own basketball practice and some wind sprints. She normally got home around midnight, where she settled in for an hour or so of study for her classes the next day. A few weeks after the start of the semester, the head coach of the girls' team quit and Pat took over. By that time she had lost 27 pounds.

Slowly and painfully, Pat's knee responded to all of her work. She was elected a cocaptain of the Olympic team and returned from Montreal with a silver medal to show her dad. The next year Pat received her master's degree and became the assistant coach of the women's basketball team at the University of Tennessee at Knoxville, the Lady Vols.

After she began coaching in Knoxville, Pat married R. B. Summitt, an area banker. They had one child, a son they named Tyler, whom his mother hopes will someday play a sport at the University of Tennessee.

Pat carried her upbringing right into her coaching style. "I've always said, 'Teams may beat us, but they better not outwork us. Coaches may beat me, but they better not outwork me.'" Pat videotapes every team practice so that she can review everyone's performance every day.

Every player on Pat's teams must attend every class and sit in the first three rows of the classroom—no excuses. Every girl who has played on a Pat Head Summitt team at the University of Tennessee for four years has graduated with a college degree—every one of them.

Giving up and accepting defeat is not allowed. Once when the team had made an especially poor showing in the second half of a game with the University of South Carolina, Pat got the team together the next afternoon back at the University of Tennessee campus. She took the still stinking uniforms from the night before from a trash can, told the girls to put them on, and then she hollered, "Now you're going to play the half you didn't play last night."

The Lady Vols won 16 games in each of the first two years Pat was a coach. Since then her teams have never won fewer than 20 games each season. For the past 17 years, the Lady Vols have played in the postseason NCAA tournament, which invites the nation's best teams to compete for the national championship. In 1987, the Lady Vols won that championship for the first time. The first thing Pat did after the game was rush into the stands for a kiss from her dad.

Pat's teams have an outstanding record in postseason tournament play, when it really counts. The Lady Vols have a 55–11 (.833) record. They have appeared as one of the final four teams 14 times and

SPORTS & ATHLETICS

Always intense during the game, Summitt refuses to let herself or her teams be outworked.

have won five national championships. In 1997, the Lady Vols won the national championship with the worst season record (29-10) of all the teams in the tournament. In 1998, they had the best record of the teams in the tournament (39-0)–and they won the championship again.

Pat's father, Richard Head, still works 10 hours a day on the family farm in Henrietta after two knee replacements, prostate surgery, two strokes, and a quadruple-bypass heart operation. He is a real fan of his daughter and her work ethic. He attends as many games as he can and has two satellite television antennas on the farm so that he can watch the games he cannot attend in person.

Another big fan of Pat's, Leon Barmore of Louisiana Tech University, coaches the team that Pat's Lady Vols beat 93-75 for the 1998 national championship at Kansas City, Missouri. He said, "Pat Summitt is, without question, the very, very best basketball coach in the women's game. I don't think there's any doubt about that. When you consider every facet: recruiting, role model, ability to coach. I think she could coach any program of any kind—men or women—and be outstanding."

CHRONOLOGY

1900	Charlotte Cooper of England wins the women's tennis competition to become the first woman to win a medal in the Olympics.
1900	Margaret Abbott becomes the first woman from the United States to win an Olympic event, golf.
1901	Cammille du Gast becomes the first woman to compete in an automobile race along with 170 men in a race between Paris and Berlin.
1926	Gertrude Ederle becomes the first woman to swim the English Channel.
1928	Betty Robinson, at the age of 16, becomes the first woman to win an Olympic gold medal in track.
1948	Alice Coachman becomes the first African-American female gold medalist in the Olympics.
1957	Althea Gibson becomes the first African-American woman to win the tennis championship at Wimbledon.
1960	Wilma Rudolph becomes the first woman to win three gold medals in track at the Olympics.
1977	Janet Guthrie becomes the first woman to race in the Indianapolis 500 race.
1984–1988	Florence Griffith Joyner wins three Olympic gold medals and one silver medal in track.
1985	Lyn St. James becomes the first woman to win a professional road race by herself.
1988	Debi Thomas becomes the first African-American woman to win a medal in Olympic ice skating.
1997	Sheryl Swoopes helps lead the Houston Comets to the first championship of the WNBA, the Women's National Basketball Association.
1998	Patricia Head Summitt coaches the University of Tennessee Lady Vols to a perfect season record (39–0) and wins the national women's college basketball championship.

FURTHER READING

Benson, Michael. *Women in Racing.* Philadelphia: Chelsea House, 1997.

Biracree, Tom. *Althea Gibson.* New York: Chelsea House, 1989.

Hunter, Shaun. *Great African Americans in the Olympics.* New York: Crabtree, 1997.

King, Billie Jean, and Cynthia Starr. *We Have Come a Long Way: The Story of Women's Tennis.* New York: McGraw-Hill, 1988.

Krull, Kathleen. *Wilma Unlimited: How Wilma Rudolph Became the World's Fastest Woman.* San Diego: Harcourt Brace, 1996.

Rediger, Pat. *Great African Americans in Sports.* New York: Crabtree, 1996.

Richardson, Ben, and William A. Fahey. *Great Black Americans.* 2d revised ed. New York: Crowell, 1976.

Wickham, Martha. *Superstars of Women's Track and Field.* Philadelphia: Chelsea House, 1997.

PHOTO CREDITS
WNBA Photos/Bill Baptist: p. 2; Archive Photos: pp. 10, 23; UPI/Corbis-Bettmann: pp. 15, 16, 26, 29, 30; Deutsche Presse Agentur/Archive Photos: p. 18; AP/Wide World Photos: pp. 12, 20, 24, 31, 45; Corbis-Bettmann/Blake Sell: p. 34; Courtesy of Janice Thomas: p. 37; Reuters/Archive Photos/Nick Didlick: p. 39; Mentor Marketing & Management/Paul Harvath: p. 40; WNBA Photos/David Liam Kyle: p. 42; AP/Wide World Photos/Susan Ragan: p. 46; AP/Wide World Photos/Alan Singer: p. 48; AP/Wide World Photos/Tim Johnson: p. 49; AP/Wide World Photos/Gene Buskar: p. 52; AP/Wide World Photos/Dave Tenenbaum: p. 56; The Photography Center/University of Tennessee: p. 58.

INDEX

Albright, Tenley, 41

Baker, Lawrence, 14
Barmore, Leon, 58–59
Baryshnikov, Mikhail, 38
Bequette, Chris, 41
Bounce Back (Swoopes), 50
Brough, Louise, 14
Brownfield High School, 44
Burt High School, 21–22

Chaffee, Nancy, 15
Charlotte World 600 race, 31
Chin, Tiffany, 37
Connolly, Maureen, 15
Conradt, Jody, 53

Eldridge, Robert, 25

Female Athlete of the Year Award, 24
Florida Agricultural and Mechanical College, 13
Fry, Shirley, 16

Gibson, Althea, 10–17
  parents of, 11
Gray, Clinton, 21–22
Guthrie, Janet, 26–33
  father of, 27

Hard, Darlene, 15
Harlem, New York, 12–13
Hazel, Richard, 53, 55, 58
Heine, Jutta, 24
Hogen, Brian Vanden, 40
Houston Comets, 43, 48–50
Hyman, Dorothy, 24

Indianapolis 500, 26, 30, 32–33
International Motor Sports Hall of Fame, 33

Jack, Hulan, 16
Jackson, Eric, 47–50
James E. Sullivan Memorial trophy, 24

Leslie, Lisa, 47
Lobo, Rebecca, 47

Marble, Alice, 13–14
McGowan, Alex, 36
McKenzie, Gordon, 30

National Association for Stock Car Racing (NASCAR), 31–32
National Tennis Championships, 14–15
Nike, Inc., 43, 47, 51
Northwestern University Medical School, 41

Olympic Games, 22–24, 35, 38–40, 47, 56
Olympic Hall of Fame (U.S.), 25

Paddleball, 12
Perez, Helen, 15
Police Athletic League, 12
Polio, 19–21

Race car driving, barriers to women in, 32
Rudolph, Wilma, 18–25
  parents of, 19–21

Sharp, Marsha, 44
South Plains College at Levelland, 44
Sports Car Club of America, 30
Stanford University, 37, 40–41
Stars on Ice, 41
Summit, Pat Head, 52–59
  parents of, 53, 55, 58
Summit, R. B., 56
Swoopes, Sheryl, 42–51
  mother of, 43

Temple, Ed, 22
Tennessee State A & I University, 22–23
Texas Tech University, 44–45
Thomas, Debi, 34–41
  mother of, 35–36
Track and Field Hall of Fame (U.S.), 25

University of Michigan, 28
University of Tennessee, 53, 55–58
University of Texas, 53
U.S. Auto Club (USAC), 30, 32
U.S. Open, 17

Vollstedt, Rolla, 31, 32

Walker, Buddy, 13
Watkins Glen race course, 30
Wilma (Rudolph), 25
Wimbledon, 10, 15–17
Witt, Katarina, 38–40
Women's National Basketball Association (WNBA), 47–49
Wooden, John, 53

ABOUT THE AUTHOR

Ann Graham Gaines is a freelance author who specializes in writing nonfiction for children. She has written a dozen books and she has master's degrees in library science and American studies from the University of Texas at Austin. She lives in the woods near Gonzales, Texas, with her four children, all readers.